Ramen Noodl

MW00990182

by Debbie Madson

www.kids-cooking-activities.com

Welcome to one of our cookbooks in our " Cooking with Kids Series"

If you have visited my website before http://www.kids-cooking-activities.com you'll know I'm a big believer in teaching kids to cook. Our slogan is **helping kids learn and grow up in the kitchen** and that is just what I'm hoping this series will interest you and your kids in doing.

Kids that learn to cook and help in the kitchen are more likely to eat what they had a hand in creating. Which means that they will be interested in trying new foods and it is a perfect opportunity to teach them new healthier options.

You can involve your kids in cooking no matter the age. We have ideas on age appropriate tasks on our site here:

http://www.kids-cooking-activities.com/kids-cooking-lessons.html

But here in this cookbook I want to share with you some fun variations on Ramen noodle recipes to get you started. There are several sections including Salads, Soups, Main Dishes and some unique ideas. We tried to include a wide range of recipes that can interest many different taste buds so I hope you find quite a few recipes that your family will enjoy.

Some tips in cooking with your kids:

- Read the recipes, ingredient lists and cooking process fully before starting
- Set out all the cooking tools

- Start with a clean workspace and stove
- Always use fresh ingredients
- Always wash your hands before cooking
- What takes an adult a short amount of time may take your child longer so be prepared

Remember to supervise your kids while they are cooking in the kitchen.

Table of Contents

Cranberry Nectarine Salad

Ingredients
1 (3-oz.) package Oriental-flavored ramen noodle
1/2 Cup dried cranberries
1 Cup hot water
1/3 Cup oil
1 Tablespoon brown sugar
2 Tablespoons balsamic vinegar
2 Tablespoons rice wine vinegar
1 Tablespoon soy sauce
package mixed salad greens
3 nectarines, peeled and cut in wedges
1 (4-oz.) package crumbled feta cheese

Directions
Cook noodles according to package directions, drain noodles and set aside. In 1 Cup of hot water, put the cranberries in, soak for 5 minutes and drain. Take the reserved flavor packet and stir in canola oil, light brown sugar, balsamic vinegar and rice wine vinegar. Stir to combine all ingredients.
Toss together in a serving bowl the ramen noodles, cranberries, gourmet greens, nectarines and feta cheese. Drizzle with dressing and toss to coat. Serve immediately.

Cabbage Salad

Ingredients
1 Cabbage, shredded or a prepared bag of coleslaw
1 pkg. chicken flavor Ramen noodles
1/4 Cup slivered almonds
1/4 Cup sunflower seeds
3-4 carrots, shredded
1 red pepper, diced
1 celery stalk, diced
Dressing:
3 Tablespoons white vinegar
3 Tablespoons white sugar
1/2 Cup canola or olive oil
seasoning packet from ramen noodles
pinch of salt and pepper

Directions
Crunch up noodles and save the flavoring for the dressing
below. In a serving bowl, add cabbage crunched noodles,
almonds, sunflower seeds and shredded carrots.
Mix salad dressing together and pour dressing over the top
right before serving. Serve immediately.

Broccoli Bacon Noodles

Ingredients
1 bunch broccoli, chopped in florets
1-2 strips of bacon or sprinkle bacon bits
1 pkg chicken or pork ramen noodles
1 Tablespoon butter

Directions
Cook noodles and drain.
Steam broccoli.
Cook bacon.
Add together cooked noodles, broccoli and bacon. Melt 1 tablespoon butter and add a dash of the noodle flavoring package. (You don't have to use it all.) Mix together and drizzle over broccoli.

Salmon Ramen Noodle Salad

Ingredients

1 package Oriental-flavored ramen noodle
1/3 pound of salmon, cut into bite size pieces
2 radishes, cut into circles
4-6 green beans, cut into bite size pieces
2 Tbsp sesame seeds
2 onions, chopped
1 bell pepper, diced
Salt and pepper to taste
1 Tbsp of honey
2 Tbsp of olive oil

Directions

Cook ramen noodles, drain and set aside.
In a pan, heat the oil and fry the salmon. Season with salt and pepper. Make sure to cook on both sides.
Now in a bowl, mix the radishes, the onion, bell pepper and the beans.
Add the noodles and salmon. Sprinkle the sesame seeds on top.
Drizzle with the honey and olive oil and toss to coat.

Mandarin Salad Oriental

Ingredients
1 (3-ounce) package Oriental-flavored ramen noodle
1/2 Cup sliced almonds
5 Tablespoons sugar, divided
1/2 Cup oil
3 Tablespoons white vinegar
1 Tablespoon fresh parsley, chopped or 1 tsp dried parsley
dash salt and pepper
dash of hot sauce
1/2 head iceberg lettuce, torn
5 celery ribs, chopped
2 green onions, chopped
small can mandarin orange sections, drained

Directions
Prepare noodles according to package directions, drain and set aside.
In a frying pan, fry the almonds and 3 tablespoons of sugar. Continually stir for 5 minutes.
Set it aside.
In a bowl, combine reserved flavor packet, 2 tablespoons sugar, oil, white vinegar, fresh parsley, hot sauce. Season with salt and pepper.
In your serving bowl, add the lettuces, celery and onions. Drizzle the liquid mixture over your salad and add the almonds and oranges. Toss to coat. Serve immediately.

Ramen Turkey Slaw

Ingredients
1 (16 oz.) pkg. shredded coleslaw mix
6 oz. cooled turkey breast, cubed
1 (3 oz.) pkg. ramen noodles
1/2 Cup vinaigrette salad dressing
1 (11 oz.) can mandarin oranges, drained well

Directions
Place the coleslaw mix into a large serving bowl.
Add the turkey and toss to combine.
Crumble the ramen noodles into the slaw and reserve the seasoning packet for another use.
Pour the dressing over the salad and toss to coat the slaw well.
Fold in the oranges.

Ramen Sweet And Tangy Coleslaw

Ingredients

2 bags coleslaw or 1 large head green cabbage, shredded
6 green onions, chopped, including tops
3/4 Cup sliced almonds, toasted
1/2 Cup sesame seeds, toasted
2 packages Ramen noodles, uncooked, crumbled slightly
1 Cup light olive oil or other salad oil
1/3 Cup rice wine vinegar
1 Tbsp sugar
2 tsp salt
1 tsp black pepper

Directions

Put coleslaw, onions, almonds, sesame seeds, and ramen noodles in large bowl and toss well.
In separate bowl, whisk together the oil, rice wine vinegar, sugar, salt, and pepper until well combined and slightly thickened.
Add just enough dressing to moisten coleslaw mixture, tossing to combine.
Serve immediately.

Soups

Spinach Ramen Soup

Ingredients

1-2 handful of baby spinach

1 pkg chicken ramen noodles

Directions

Cook noodles according to directions. Add in seasoning. Once noodles are tender add in baby spinach. Once spinach starts to wilt, serve.

Ramen Noodle Wonton Soup

Ingredients
1 package Oriental-flavored ramen noodle
Wonton wrappers
1/2 pound of small shrimp
8-10 green pea pods, diced finely
2 onions, chopped
1 bell pepper, diced finely
Salt and pepper to taste
6 Cups broth
2 Tbsp olive oil
1 tsp oregano

Directions
In a pan, heat the oil and fry the chopped onions.
Fry the shrimp for 2 minutes. Then add the peas.
Season with salt and pepper and stir for 30 seconds. Take off heat.
Allow to cool slightly.
Lay a wonton wrapper flat in your hand and add a spoonful of shrimp mixture.
Wet edges of wrapper with water on your finger.
Lift edges to opposite corner, making a triangle and press to seal. Continue with wrappers until mixture is used up.
In a soup pot, add in the broth, oregano, ramen noodles and add the wontons gently to the broth.
Cover and cook for 15-20 minutes.
Serve hot

Chinese Noodles

Ingredients
2 chicken flavor noodles
3 Cups water
rotisserie chicken, shredded
6-8 shrimp
1 cup shredded cabbage
3 Tbsp. soy sauce

Directions
Cook noodles and stir in flavoring packets.   Stir in chicken, shrimp, cabbage and soy sauce to soup. Cook several minutes until cabbage is wilted.

Ramen Noodle and Crab soup

Ingredients
1 package Oriental-flavored ramen noodle
1/3 pound of imitation crab meat
2 leeks, chopped
1 carrots, sliced
4 green beans, diced
1 bell pepper, diced
Salt to taste
4 Cups broth
1 tsp parsley

Directions
Add noodles and seasoning packet into a large soup pan, add in leeks, noodles, carrots, green beans, bell peppers and broth. Season with salt and pepper and parsley. Cook 10 minutes or until vegetables are tender. Add in crab meat. Heat and serve.

Ramen Chicken Veggie Soup

Ingredients
1 package Oriental-flavored ramen noodle with flavoring packet
1/3 pound of chicken, diced
1/2 of cauliflower head, diced
2 carrots, diced or shredded
2 onions, chopped
1 bell pepper, diced
can green beans, drained
Salt and pepper to taste
4 cup of chicken broth
1 tsp of oregano

Directions
In a soup pot, add diced chicken, cauliflower, carrots, onions, diced peppers, green beans, chicken broth and noodles. Stir in flavoring packet, oregano and add a sprinkle of salt and pepper. Cook 15-20 minutes until chicken is tender.
Taste and season with more oregano, salt and pepper, if needed.

Easy Ramen Noodle Veggie Soup

Ingredients
2 tsp vegetable oil
1 lb boneless beef sirloin steak, cut thin strips
2 Cups water
1 package (3 oz) Oriental-flavor ramen noodle soup mix
1 pkg (1 lb) frozen stir-fry vegetables
1/4 Cup stir-fry sauce

Directions
Heat the oil and cook the beef for 3 to 5 minutes. Remove and set aside for now.
Add water and bring it to boiling.
Add the ramen noodles in and wait for them to get soft.
Add the vegetables. Boil for 5 minutes.
Add seasoning packet to noodles. Add stir-fry sauce and the beef.
Cook several minutes until heated through.

Corn Chowder Noodle Soup

Ingredients
1 pkg chicken ramen noodles
1 can cream corn
1 1/2 Cups water
bacon bits

Directions
In a soup pot, add Ramen noodles, cream of corn and water. Cook until noodles are tender. Serve with a sprinkle of bacon bits.

Mushroom and Ramen noodle soup

Ingredients
1 package Oriental-flavored ramen noodle
1 cup of brown mushrooms, sliced
2 onions, chopped
Salt and pepper to taste
4 Cups of beef broth
2 Tbsp of olive oil
1 tsp oregano or parsley
red pepper, diced, if desired

Directions
In a soup pan, heat the oil and fry the onion and continue with the mushrooms.
Add in oregano, ramen flavoring packet, salt and pepper.
Pour in the broth.
Now add the ramen noodles.
Cover and cook for 10 minutes.

Mushroom Ramen Soup

Ingredients
1 pack of instant ramen noodles - any flavor
4 carrots, cut into circles
4 Cups of chicken broth
1/2 Cup white mushrooms, sliced
4 green pea pods, diced
1 Tbsp cooking oil
2 Tbsp parsley, finely chopped or 1 tsp. dried parsley
Salt and pepper to taste

Directions
In a skillet, heat the oil and fry mushrooms.
Add the peas and carrots. Stir for 2 minutes.
Season with salt and pepper. Add the broth and stir.
Add in the ramen noodles and cover.
Cook for about 15 minutes or until carrots are tender.
Add the parsley. Serve hot

Egg Drop Ramen Soup

Ingredients
1 packet ramen soup
1 egg, beaten
1 green onion or chives, diced
5-6 spinach leaves, optional
1 tsp. sesame oil

Directions
Cook ramen noodles in a soup pan according to directions, using the flavoring packet. When noodles are tender add in spinach leaves and green onions. Once spinach begins to wilt. Stir in a beaten egg and stir around with a fork. Drizzle with sesame oil and serve.

Main Dishes

Snap Pea Stir-Fry

Ingredients
1-pound sugar snap peas
3 tablespoons vegetable oil
1-pound boneless sirloin steak, sliced thin
2 tablespoons fresh chopped ginger or 1 tsp. ground ginger
2 garlic cloves, minced
3 green onions, diced
1 Cup beef broth
1/4 Cup soy sauce
2 Tablespoons cornstarch
1 Tablespoon sesame oil
2 packages ramen noodles, save flavorings for another day

Directions
Prepare noodles as per directions on the package. Drain and set aside. Save the seasoning packet to add to the sauce.
Boil your snap peas. Drain, and set aside.
Heat only 1 Tablespoon of oil in a pan. Add the sirloin steak. Toss for 2 minutes. Set aside for now.
Add 2 Tbsp. vegetable oil to your skillet. Add ginger, if using fresh, garlic cloves and scallions.
Stir and cook one minute.
In a bowl, pour in the beef broth, seasoning packet and the soy sauce. Whisk in 2 Tbsp. of cornstarch. Pour beef broth, peas and steak into skillet. Add sesame oil. Stir in your cooked ramen noodles (without flavorings). Toss to coat and serve hot.

Ramen Noodle Stir-Fry with Chicken and Vegetables

Ingredients
1 package Oriental-flavored ramen noodle
1/4-pound beef
8-10 green pea pods, diced
1/2 Cup of broccoli, diced
2 red onions, chopped
2 bell peppers, diced
2 Tbsp. soy sauce
1/2 tsp pepper
Salt to taste
2 Tbsp olive oil

Directions
Boil the noodles, drain and set aside. Save the seasoning packet. In a pan, heat the oil and fry the beef for 5 minutes. Add in the broccoli, diced peppers and green peas. Season with salt and pepper and cook for 5 more minutes. Add 2 Tablespoons soy sauce and the seasoning packet to your vegetables.
Add the cooked noodles and stir all to combine.
~ You can substitute one bag of frozen stir fry vegetables for the broccoli, peppers and peas.

Beef Ramen Noodle

Ingredients
1 package Oriental-flavored ramen noodle
1/3-pound ground beef
8-10 green pea pods, diced
2 onions, chopped
1 bell pepper, diced
Salt and pepper to taste
1/2 Cup of beef broth
2 Tbsp of olive oil
1 tsp of oregano

Directions
Cook ramen noodles, drain and set aside.
In a pan, heat the oil and fry the onions.
Add the beef and fry for about 5 minutes or until no longer pink. Drain grease off meat and add back to pan.
Add the peas into the beef mixture.
Season with salt and pepper.
Now add the cooked ramen noodles on top and add the oregano.
Pour the beef broth on top.
Cover and cook for about 10 min, Serve hot

Ramen Omelet

Ingredients
1 package of instant ramen noodles - any flavor
1 Tbsp oil
2 Tbsp onion, finely chopped, if desired
1/2 Cup cherry tomatoes, halved
2 Tbsp parsley, finely chopped or 1 T. dried parsley
2 eggs

Directions
Boil your ramen noodles, drain and set aside. Reserve the flavoring for another time.
Heat the oil in a pan and fry chopped onions for 2 minutes. Add in the noodles and the chopped parsley.
Spread all of it evenly on the pan covering the bottom of the pan.
Beat the eggs with a pinch of salt. Now pour egg mixture on top of your noodles.
Cook for 4 minutes. Flip over and cook on the other side 1-2 minutes.

Coconut & Nuts Ramen

Ingredients
1 pack of instant ramen noodles - any flavor
1 cabbage, chopped
4 Tbsp of shredded coconut
3 Tbsp olive oil
1/2 Cup walnut, chopped
1/2 Cup cashew nuts, chopped
4 onions, finely chopped
2 green chilies, chopped, optional
Fresh coriander, chopped
Salt to taste
Pepper to taste

Directions
Boil the ramen noodles for 2 minutes and drain. Set aside.
In a large bowl, add the cabbage, diced onions, chopped chilies and coriander.
Throw in the nuts and stir.
Add the ramen noodles and shredded coconut.
Season with salt and pepper. Drizzle with olive oil and give it a final toss to coat.

~Be careful chopping chilies. It is best to use plastic gloves.

Ramen Noodle Pepperoni Pizza

Ingredients
1 pack of instant ramen noodles
1/4- 1/2 Cup shredded mozzarella cheese
3 Tbsp olive oil
5-6 Pepperoni slices
Salt to taste
Pepper to taste

Directions
Preheat the oven to 350F or 180C. Boil the noodles for 2 minutes and drain.
Grease a pizza tray with oil or use cooking spray.
Flatten the ramen noodles flat like a pizza crust.
Sprinkle cheese on top and add the pepperoni. Season with salt and pepper
Bake for 5-8 minutes.
Serve hot.

Ramen Noodle Taco

Ingredients
1 pack of instant ramen noodles
2 taco shells
2 tbsp olive oil
cooked ground beef
refried beans
shredded cheese
chopped tomatoes or salsa

Directions
In a skillet, deep fry the ramen noodles in the 2
Tablespoons oil and break them into little pieces.
To assemble your tacos, add your desired taco toppings
such as refried beans, ground beef, fried noodles, cheese
and salsa.

You can top it off with sour cream or guacamole.

Lettuce Wraps

Ingredients
shredded chicken, use rotisserie chicken works great
iceberg lettuce
Ramen noodles
shredded carrots

Directions
Wash and carefully take lettuce leaves apart. Allow to dry while you prepare the meal. Break your ramen noodles into small pieces and cook according to package directions. Drain.
To serve, place a lettuce leaf on your plate and add shredded chicken, noodles and shredded carrots. Wrap up your lettuce and eat.

Chili Ramen

Ingredients
1 can of chili
1/2 Cup shredded cheddar cheese
1 pkg beef noodles

Directions
Prepare ramen noodles according to package directions. Warm chili. To serve, add noodles to each plate and add a scoop of chili and sprinkle with cheese.

Ramen Noodle Burgers

Ingredients

1 package Oriental-flavored ramen noodle soup mix
2 hamburger or veggie patties
mixed greens
Salt and pepper to taste
1 tbsp of olive oil

Directions

Boil the noodles and drain. Let it cool. Bake or grill your hamburgers until they are done.
In a pan heat the oil, fry the noodles in batches forming into a patty.
Make sure you make a shape that perfectly substitutes for the burger's buns.
Serve with your ramen noodle "buns", burger and your mixed greens.

Ramen Noodle Dog

Ingredients
1 package Oriental-flavored ramen noodle reserve flavoring for another day
A handful of spinach, optional
2 sausages or hot dogs
1 tsp of pepper
2 Tbsp of olive oil

Directions
Boil the ramen noodles and drain. Set aside and let it cool.
In a pan, heat the oil and fry the sausage or hot dogs.
Take off the heat, fry the spinach for 30 seconds and take off the heat.
Set spinach aside.
Now fry the ramen noodles for 5 minutes
Plate it up with the noodles, sausage and spinach. Serve hot.

Noodles and Cheese

Ingredients
1 slice American cheese
1 packet ramen noodles

Directions
Cook ramen according to directions. Drain and immediately add cheese while noodles are hot. Stir to combine cheese.

~A fun variation on Macaroni and cheese.

Ramen Ham Cheese Cups

Ingredients

1 package ramen noodle any flavor reserve the flavoring
for another time
1/2 Cup shredded cheese
diced ham or sliced ham cut into small pieces
Salt and pepper to taste
2 tbsp of olive oil

Directions

Grease a muffin tray with oil.
Boil your ramen noodles for only 1 minute and drain.
Add ramen noodles in the muffin tray, pushing up against
the sides. Sprinkle each cup with shredded cheese and
diced ham.
Season with salt and pepper.
Bake for 10 minutes or until cheese is melted in a 350F or
180 C oven

Beef Carrot Ramen

Ingredients
1 package Oriental-flavored ramen noodle with flavoring packet
1/3-pound beef, cut into bite size pieces, optional
2 green onions, chopped
2 carrots, diced
Salt and pepper to taste
1 Cup beef broth
2 Tbsp olive oil
1 tsp oregano

Directions
In a large skillet or wok, add all ingredients. Cook on medium heat and simmer 15-20 minutes until beef is cooked and vegetables are tender.

Ramen Noodle with Shrimp Gravy

Ingredients
1 package Oriental-flavored ramen noodle
1/3-pound shrimp
1 Cup coconut milk
1/2 Cup fresh cream
A handful of collard leaves
8-10 green pea pods, diced
2 onions, chopped
salt and pepper to taste
4 Cups broth
2 Tbsp olive oil
1 tsp oregano

Directions
In a large skillet or wok, heat the oil. Fry the onions several minutes.
Add in the shrimp and peas. Season with salt and pepper and oregano.
Pour in the coconut milk and cream, stir.
Finally add the broth
Cover and cook for about 30 minutes.

Chicken Pad Thai Casserole

Ingredients

4 cups diced cooked chicken
1 pack (3 oz) Oriental Ramen noodles, broken up slightly
1 can (28 oz) chop suey vegetables
1 cup water stir in noodle flavoring packet

Directions

Preheat oven to 350 degrees. Lightly oil a casserole dish.
Put all the ingredients together in a large bowl and toss to
combine well, then pour into casserole dish.
Cover tightly and bake in preheated oven for 30 to 40
minutes or until bubbly hot and ramen noodles are tender.

Chef Salad Ramen

Ingredients
Ramen noodles chicken flavor

1-2 boiled eggs

cooked sliced chicken breast

shredded or chopped carrots

1-2 bacon slices, cooked

other vegetables of your choice

Directions
Prepare noodles adding seasoning packet and drain. Add to large bowl and top with remaining salad ingredients.

Easy Thai Noodles

Ingredients
1 pkg Asian ramen noodles

1-2 Cups fresh green beans snapped in pieces

1-2 carrots, diced

1 green onion, diced

1 Tablespoon peanut butter

Directions
Cook noodles according to directions on package, drain and set aside. In skillet or wok, stir fry fresh green beans, diced green onion and diced carrots. Add in cooked noodles, seasoning packet and 1 Tablespoon peanut butter. Cook until vegetables are tender.

Easy Hamburger Noodle Helper

Ingredients
Ramen noodles, crunched up
2 cans of diced tomatoes or 5-6 fresh diced
1 can of corn or 2 Cups frozen corn
1 lb. ground beef or ground chicken

Directions
In skillet, brown beef or chicken and drain if needed. Stir in tomatoes, corn, seasoning packet and noodles. Cover and let boil until liquid goes down.

Easy Ramen Chicken Parmesan

Ingredients
frozen chicken nuggets or chicken patties
spaghetti sauce
1 pkg chicken flavored ramen noodles
1/2 Cup mozzarella cheese

Directions
Boil noodles and add seasoning packet. Meanwhile, cook chicken nuggets in oven according to directions. To serve, add 1/2 Cup noodles to plate, top with chicken patty or several chicken nuggets. Then add a spoonful of sauce on top of the chicken and sprinkle with mozzarella cheese. If you'd like the cheese melted, place in microwave for 1 minute or until melted.

Misc. Ramen Recipes

Taco Ramen Snack Mix

Ingredients
3 Cups baked cheese crackers
2 Cups butter flavored pretzel sticks
1 pkg crunched up ramen noodles, save the flavoring for another time
1 Tablespoon of vegetable oil
2 Tablespoons of dry taco seasoning mix

Directions
Place the crackers in a large microwave safe mixing bowl.
Add the pretzels and peanuts and gently toss to combine.
Drizzle the oil over the top and stir with a spoon to evenly coat.
Sprinkle with the taco seasoning mix and stir again to coat well.
Microwave the mixture on high for 2 minutes.
Remove and stir with a wooden spoon.
Return to the microwave and heat for an additional 2 minutes on high.
Allow the mix to stand 5 minutes before serving.

~Experiment with different flavorings such as substituting taco seasoning mix with ranch dressing mix or a flavoring packet.

Ramen Chocolates

Ingredients
12 oz of chocolate chips or white chocolate chips
2-3 pkg ramen noodles, crunched up

Directions
Melt chocolate in a microwave safe bowl in 1-minute intervals, stirring after each minute until melted. Stir in crunched up ramen noodles. Place spoonfuls onto a waxed paper lined cookie sheet. Chill in the fridge several hours.

What to do with those leftover flavoring packets

- Add to water that you are cooking rice in

- Add to meatloaf

- Add 1 packet to 2 cups hot water for a broth

- Thicken above mixture with 1 T. cornstarch for a gravy to top cube steak, hamburgers, etc.

Made in the USA
San Bernardino, CA
23 March 2019